The Coral Necklace

Published in 2023

Printed in the USA.

Written by Shanti Ghosh, illustrated by Shanti Ghosh, graphic design by Sona Agarwal.
Text edited by Alia Einstein Diez.

www.sahajabooksforchildren.com

The Coral Necklace

The Coral Necklace story is based on Shri Mataji's lecture on 19th May, 1985, Shri Ganesha Puja, Rome, Italy. In this talk Shri Mataji can be seen wearing the necklace about which this story is written.

written and illustrated by Shanti Ghosh

Many years ago in Italy, there lived a jeweler named Gianni. He was a simple, honest man who took great pride in his work. The most notable thing about Gianni was that he could feel God's love in his heart when most people were blind to such things. Gianni dared not speak of this to the people around him, for they might think him mad and laugh at him. Instead, he allowed this love to flow through him to make the most beautiful jewelry pieces.

Gianni lived in Genoa, a beautiful Italian town on the shores of the Ligurian Sea. While he was strolling on the beach, he saw a lovely red coral on display in one of the sea-side stalls. He felt a rush of cool vibrations, and without a thought, he bought it. Filled with excitement, he hurried back to his workshop to start work on his next project.

Gianni spent many hours delicately carving the coral into twelve perfect beads. He decorated each bead with beautiful designs, pouring his love into this work. Finally, he strung ten beads together to make a necklace and used the remaining two beads to create matching earrings.

He reluctantly decided to sell the beautiful necklace, displaying it in his mall shop window.

Despite his brilliance, Gianni was poor. When he needed money to buy warm clothes and food for winter, he reluctantly decided to sell the beautiful necklace, displaying it in his small shop window. A few weeks passed...

One cool, sunny autumn day, a wealthy Indian trader called Ajay strolled through the quaint local market in Genoa, looking for gifts to take to India. He scanned all the pretty shop displays as he walked, but Gianni's stunning necklace caught his eye - Ajay entered Gianni's shop to take a closer look.

Upon entering, Ajay could see each of the rings, bracelets, and necklaces had been beautifully handcrafted with great care and love. Nothing, however, compared with that red necklace set in the window. Ajay was sure it would make a perfect gift for his younger sister and immediately bought it.

woof
woof

On arriving back in India, Ajay was so eager to give his sister the necklace that he did not even wait for his usual driver, instead, rushing into the first available rickshaw. When he reached his sister's house, in haste, he climbed out of the rickshaw but tripped.

The necklace in its small carry pouch slipped out of his bag, landing somewhere on the seat of the rickshaw, which then sped off down the busy street before Ajay even realized that the necklace was missing.

The next passenger to ride that rickshaw happened to be another jeweler named Hari, who immediately noticed and then opened the pouch to find Gianni's beautiful necklace set. Hari studied the beautiful designs on the coral beads of the necklace. He was so inspired that when he reached his jewelry store, he immediately started working on a matching mangalsutra.

Some time passed... and in early 1985, a group of Australian yogis was blessed with an opportunity to go shopping with Shri Mataji in India. They wanted to buy a mangalsutra for Shri Mataji, but as they walked through the market streets, they found all the jewelry shops closed. Disappointed, they began to turn back when suddenly, Shri Mataji felt tremendous vibrations coming from a small shop at the end

of the street. A few yogis followed the cool vibrations into the store, astonished to find Gianni's beautiful coral necklace set and Hari's matching mangalsutra. "How auspicious," said Shri Mataji, explaining that coral is the stone of Shri Ganesha and that Australian yogis are his ganas. The yogis were delighted to have found

such a gift so spontaneously and bought the mangalstutra and the coral necklace set to tale back to Australia. They planned to present them to Shri Mataji at the next puja in London, England.

Back in an Australian ashram, the mangalsutra and the necklace set were carefully packed in a box ready to be taken to London. But when it was time to leave for Londo, OH NO! No one could find the box! The yogis searched every-where without success...

the jewelry disappeared!

One beautiful day in May of that same year, an Australian yogini, Thelma, was cleaning up the altar in the Australian ashram when she noticed a beautifully wrapped jewelry box placed at the feet of Shri Ganesha's statue. Curiously, she picked it up to see what was inside.

Lo and behold.

She found the coral necklace set!

It looked like Shri Ganesha had kept them hidden until that very moment. It was almost time for Shri Ganesha puja in Italy. Thelma took the jewelry with her and presented it to Shri Mataji at Shri Ganesha puja.

When Shri Mataji wore the coral necklace for the Ganesha puja, she explained: "This is Ritambara Pragnya!" (Mother nature). "See, all of this was to happen. The ganas from Australia has sent this coral necklace to the Devas of Europe to be worn at Shri Ganesha Puja. The ten stones represent the dharma or guru principle of Europe, and with the earings, there are twelve stones that represent the heart in England, and all of you are represented here today.

What a blessig! Now, the necklace I made is being worn by the Adi Shakti herself.

Gianni was no longer alive by the time the necklace reached its ultimate destination. But his spirit was present at the puja, surely overjoyed in seeing his creation worn by Shri Mataji. His purest desire to make a necklace for god was fulfilled at last. Everything worked out according to god's plans. Gianni's necklace traveled around the world, spreading cool vibrations until it made it's way back to Italy, where it was worn by the Adi Shakti.

at the most auspicious time.

"Now you should be able to read through the beautiful working of Ritambhara Pragnya, which is very subtle and then you will start enjoying the littlem little things it plays to make you very happy and to fulfil your deisres."
- Shri Mataji Nirmala Devi, Shri Ganesh Puja, Rome 1985